FARM EXPLORER

Can Robots Milk Cows?

QUESTIONS AND ANSWERS ABOUT FARM MACHINES

by Katherine Rawson

CAPSTONE PRESS
a capstone imprint

Published by Pebble Sprout, an imprint of Capstone.
1710 Roe Crest Drive, North Mankato, Minnesota 56003
capstonepub.com

Library of Congress Cataloging-in-Publication Data is available on the Library of Congress website.
ISBN: 9781666349214 (hardcover)
ISBN: 9781666349252 (paperback)
ISBN: 9781666349290 (ebook PDF)

Summary:
Tractors, wagons, combines, and trailers—what are these things? They're all machines on a farm! How do they work? What are they for? Kids can get to know the many machines that make farms go in this interactive Pebble Sprout series.

Editorial Credits:
Editor: Kristen Mohn; Designer: Sarah Bennett; Media Researcher: Julie De Adder; Production Specialist: Katy LaVigne

Image Credits:
Dreamstime: Dmitry Kalinovsky, 28; Getty Images: esvetleishaya, 29 (back), EThamPhoto, 30, Fei Yang, 17, Joseph Sohm, 22, Manu_Bahuguna, 27, PeopleImages, 5, PolakPhoto, 32 (bottom left); Shutterstock: Africa Studio, cover (cow), Air Images, cover (bottom right), Earl D. Walker, 3 (top left), Emily Li, 20 (bottom), Eric Isselee, 25 (lamb), Florin Cnejevici, 3 (middle right), Fotokostic, 15 (bottom), Gelpi, 4, Harald Lueder, 15 (top), Javier Brosch, 23 (towel), Kitja Kitja, 6 (bottom), Kletr, 13, kreatorex, cover (bottom left), Lurin, 8, Mai.Chayakorn, 24, Mauro Rodrigues (robot), cover, 29, Milkovasa, 19 (farmer), mipan, 21 (wagon), muratart, 12 (middle), newelle, 23 (hands), Olga Pasynkova (background), back cover and throughout, Operation Shooting, 25 (barber chair), oticki, 6 (top), 19 (field), Phonkrit Ninchak, 32 (top), Photoagriculture, 3 (top middle and middle), photomaster, 31 (top), photostar72, 3 (top right), Pineapple studio, 23 (egg), piscary, 14, Ratikova, 20 (top), Ratthaphong Ekariyasap, 3 (middle left), Real Vector, 11 (watering can), Roman Pelesh (bucket), cover, 29, Ronaldo Almeida, 32 (bottom right), rsooll, 7 (field), Scharfsinn, 18, schwarzhana, 10 (bottom), Serg64, 11 (field), smereka, 10 (top), 16 (bottom), 31 (bottom right), StockStudio Aerials, 3 (bottom left), Suzanne Tucker, 9, tanger, cover (bottom middle), teamplay, 12 (water drops), Terelyuk, 26, TFoxFoto, 31 (bottom left), Thomas Soellner, 7 (tape measure), Wanderlust Media, 3 (bottom right), Yevgen Kravchenko, 23 (brush and bubbles), 24 (bubbles), YummyBuum, 23 (face), Zaharia Bogdan Rares, 21 (peanut), ZhakYaroslav, 16 (top)

Farmers have many different kinds of machines to help them do their work. Machines help farmers plant and harvest crops. They help feed and care for animals. They help move things around the farm.

Let's find out about the different things farm machines can do. Read each question and try to guess the answer. Then turn the page to find out.

Did you guess right?

What does a tractor do?

A tractor helps with just about every job on a farm. It pulls equipment for plowing, planting, and harvesting.

Tractors help stack hay bales and move crops to storage. Without tractors, many farm jobs would be hard to do.

How do farmers make straight rows in fields?

Farmers use a machine called a plow to prepare their fields for crops. A plow has blades that loosen the ground before planting, break up weeds, and mix fertilizer into the soil.

All these things help the seeds grow better.

Corn planter machines plant many rows of corn at a time. They make furrows, drop the seeds in, and cover them with dirt.

Depending on their size, the machines can plant up to 48 rows of corn all at once!

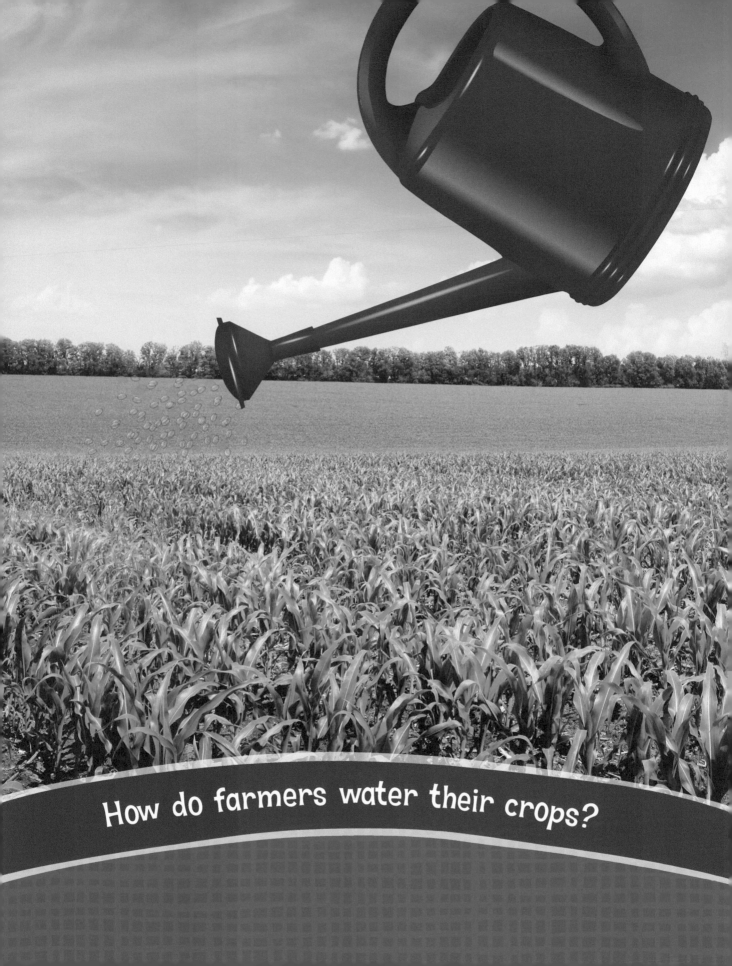

How do farmers water their crops?

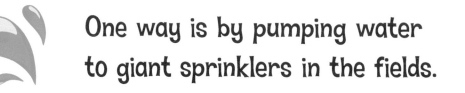

One way is by pumping water to giant sprinklers in the fields.

The sprinklers have wheels and can move around to water all parts of a field.

Does a combine combine things?

The machine called a combine doesn't combine *things*—it combines jobs!

Harvesting grain takes several steps. The combine does them all. In just one trip across the field, it cuts the plant, separates the grain, cleans the grain, and collects it.

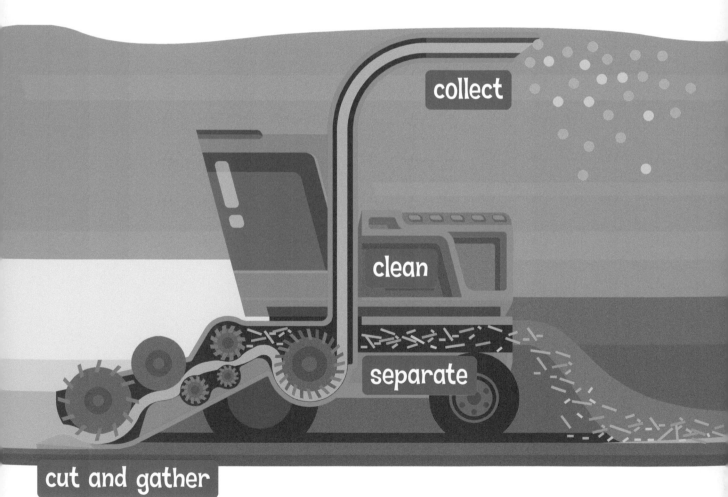

Is a hay mower like a lawn mower?

A hay mower is much larger than a lawn mower, and it is pulled by a tractor.

After the cut hay has dried, the tractor pulls a large rake to gather the hay into rows. Then a machine called a baler makes the hay into bales.

Can machines pick fruit?

Yes! Some machines have robotic arms that pluck the fruit from trees or stems.

Other machines shake the plants so that the fruit falls off. Machines can pick a lot of fruit in a short amount of time.

How do farmers get
potatoes out of the ground?

For large fields, farmers use a potato harvester. This machine lifts potatoes out of the ground and cuts them from the vines. Some potato harvesters are pulled by tractors, and some move on their own. They can harvest several rows at once.

A peanut wagon is a large trailer for drying peanuts after they are harvested. Warm air blows over the peanuts for several days until they are completely dry. Drying keeps the peanuts from spoiling.

They go through an egg washing machine. Brushes gently scrub off the dirt and straw, and water rinses them clean.

Some machines can wash thousands of eggs per hour!

How do sheep get haircuts?

Cutting the wool off sheep is called shearing. The electric clippers used to give sheep haircuts are called shearing machines. They are similar to the clippers used for people's haircuts.

BEEP!
BEEP!

Backhoes can go forward or backward! A backhoe pulls its shovel back to scoop things rather than pushing forward, like a snow shovel.

Farmers use backhoes to dig holes, pull out stumps, or move heavy rocks around. Backhoes help with all kinds of big jobs on the farm.

Can robots milk cows?

Yes! Some farms use robotic milking systems. When a cow enters the milking parlor, a robotic arm cleans her udder and attaches the milking machine. When milking is done, the robot removes the machine and the cow *moo*-ves on with her day.

Fun Farm Facts!

Some hay balers make square bales and some make round bales. Square bales weigh about 50 pounds (23 kilograms) each. Round bales are much larger and can weigh as much as 1,000 pounds (454 kg)!

One type of machine used for harvesting blueberries is an over-the-row harvester. It is tall enough to fit over a row of blueberry bushes. It moves down the row, shaking the bushes so that the berries fall off into the bottom of the harvester.

Corn planters are fast. The larger ones can plant 35 acres (14 hectares) or more in just one hour. That's almost the size of 20 professional soccer fields!

Hens usually lay one egg a day, but they take time off now and then. The average hen lays around 300 eggs in a year. That's a lot of eggs to wash!

Many farmers hire professional shearers to shear their sheep. An experienced shearer can shear a sheep in just a few minutes. The world record for shearing one sheep is 37.9 seconds.

It takes up to 30 minutes for a person to milk a cow. A milking machine can do it in 5 to 8 minutes.